From Antietam to Gettysburg
A Civil War Coloring Book

PETER F. COPELAND

Dover Publications, Inc., New York

*For Christina Desiré Klinger,
whose ancestor, Private Walton Coffman,
Company E, Eleventh Virginia Cavalry,
was killed at Fisher's Hill, Virginia.*

Introduction

This book will show and describe the two Confederate invasions of the North undertaken by Robert E. Lee's Army of Northern Virginia. The purpose of these campaigns was both political and military; the objective of carrying the war into the enemy's country was important in Lee's planning. Both the Northern and Southern armies, campaigning across Virginia, were reducing great areas of that Confederate state to near-exhaustion and starvation. Soldiers of both armies carried off livestock and horses, burned and seized crops and ravaged farmland all over northern Virginia. The battles fought over Richmond were destroying her towns and villages. Maryland and Pennsylvania, on the other hand, had not been fought over. Their farmlands and industries promised a rich reward to the Confederate army, which was always in need of food, clothing and supplies.

The first Southern invasion ended in the bloody battle of Antietam, called Sharpsburg by the Southerners, a terrible contest fought on September 17, 1862. It was a victory for neither side, and the end of the campaign saw the Union army, led by General George B. McClellan, holding its positions while the outnumbered Army of Northern Virginia retreated, exhausted, back into Virginia.

It was nearly two months before the Federal Army of the Potomac, now led by General Ambrose E. Burnside, advanced again against Richmond, aiming to seize the town of Fredericksburg, Virginia, on the Rappahannock river. The result of this campaign was the disastrous battle of Fredericksburg, fought December 12 and 13, 1862, in which the Union army was defeated, losing over twelve thousand men.

General Joseph "Fighting Joe" Hooker led the Army of the Potomac into another terrible defeat at Chancellorsville, May 2 and 3, 1863, losing approximately seventeen thousand men before Lee decided to mount another invasion of the North, this time without the invaluable assistance of Stonewall Jackson, who died of wounds received at Chancellorsville.

As Lee moved his army northward toward Pennsylvania, General Jeb Stuart, Confederate cavalry leader, fought an indecisive saber-swinging horseman's battle with Federal General Alfred Pleasanton at Brandy Station, Virginia.

Lee marched through Maryland and entered Pennsylvania in late June of 1863. The battle of Gettysburg was a three-day affair, July 1–3, that produced over fifty-one thousand casualties before it ended. On the last day, July 3, Confederate General George Pickett led fifteen thousand Southern soldiers in a frontal attack against Union artillery and riflemen on Cemetery Ridge, and was turned back with heavy losses.

The next day Lee commenced a retreat into Virginia and the last large-scale Confederate invasion of the North was over.

PETER COPELAND

Published in Canada by General Publishing Company, Ltd., 30 Lesmill Road, Don Mills, Toronto, Ontario. Published in the United Kingdom by Constable and Company, Ltd.

From Antietam to Gettysburg: A Civil War Coloring Book is a new work, first published by Dover Publications, Inc., in 1983.

DOVER *Pictorial Archive* SERIES

This book belongs to the Dover Pictorial Archive Series. You may use the designs and illustrations for graphics and crafts applications, free and without special permission, provided that you include no more than four in the same publication or project. (For permission for additional use, please write to Dover Publications, Inc., 31 East 2nd Street, Mineola, N.Y. 11501.)

However, republication or reproduction of any illustration by any other graphic service, whether it be in a book or in anyother design resource, is strictly prohibited.

International Standard Book Number: 0-486-24476-8

Manufactured in the United States of America.
Dover Publications, Inc., 31 East 2nd Street, Mineola, N.Y. 11501

1. Robert E. Lee's Army Crossing the Potomac and Entering Maryland, September 1862. The Confederate Army of Northern Virginia crossed the Potomac at White's Ford on a late summer afternoon, the soldiers singing "Maryland, My Maryland" in the belief that the people of that state would rise up and join the Southern cause.

2. Sharpsburg, Maryland, September 1862. Though few recruits joined him in Maryland, Lee advanced with forty thousand men to occupy the town of Frederick and headed toward Hagerstown. Informed that the enemy had captured a copy of his orders to the army, Lee retreated to the village of Sharpsburg and decided to fight the Union army on Antietam Creek.

3. General George B. McClellan. An expert at organizing, training and supplying an army, McClellan, commander of the Army of the Potomac, was no match for Lee as a general on the battlefield. He was indecisive and faltering in his management of battle and, even with an army of ninety thousand men and a copy of Lee's secret orders, he could not crush the Southern army at Antietam.

4. Union Attack at Burnside Bridge, September 17, 1862. On the left of the Union line, the men of General Ambrose Burnside's corps gallantly stormed across Antietam Creek over a narrow stone bridge into the teeth of heavy Confederate fire.

5. Federal Attack on Jackson's Line through a Cornfield. General Joseph Hooker's troops, after assaulting Stonewall Jackson's positions in the East Woods on the Confederate left on September 16, renewed their attack through a cornfield early on the seventeenth and pressed the Confederates to retreat.

6. Counterattack by Hood's Division, September 17, 1862. The retreating Southern soldiers were rallied by General Lee himself, and rushed forward in a desperate counterattack. The fighting surged back and forth through the day until the green corn was trampled and spattered with blood.

7. Union Signal Tower on Elk Mountain. Northern artillery at Antietam was deadly, directed by signalmen on Elk Mountain who had an effective overview of the Confederate positions and communicated with their gunners by signal flag.

8. The Townspeople of Sharpsburg Aid in Caring for the Wounded after the Battle of Antietam. The battle ended in a bloody stalemate, and the fields of Antietam were littered with the bodies of the dead and wounded. The Union army medical corpsmen were aided by civilian volunteers from the neighborhood in getting the wounded to the surgeons' lines.

9. Lincoln Meets McClellan at the Headquarters of the Army of the Potomac. Lee retreated back into Virginia after Antietam and the commander of the Army of the Potomac, despite urgent pleas from President Abraham Lincoln, made no effort to follow him. On October 3, 1862, the President visited McClellan's camp to urge the General to resume his march upon Richmond, the Confederate capital.

10. Confederate Cavalry Raiding Chambersburg, Pennsylvania, October 10, 1862. Unopposed by the slow-moving Union army, eighteen hundred cavalrymen of the Army of Northern Virginia raided the town of Chambersburg in Pennsylvania, where they burned stores of Federal army clothing and weapons.

11. General Ambrose E. Burnside. The Chambersburg raid finally convinced President Lincoln that he must replace General McClellan with a more active and resourceful commander. General Burnside, who had fought so gallantly at Antietam, was chosen as the new commander of the Army of the Potomac. Though a popular officer with the army, Burnside himself knew that he was not equal to the task.

12. Federal Troops Preparing to Cross the Rappahannock River at Fredericksburg, Virginia, December 11, 1862. Burnside planned a surprise attack upon the town of Fredericksburg and a dash from there to Richmond. It was with difficulty that the Union army got across the Rappahannock in the face of heavy Confederate fire from the defenders of the town. Lee had not been surprised. The Army of Northern Virginia had made a fortress of Fredericksburg.

13. Confederate Troops Repelling the Federal Attack on Marye's Heights. Once across the river the Union army had to storm entrenched Confederate positions on Marye's Heights before Fredericksburg. Southern rifle fire and artillery shattered line after line of Northern attackers. That evening the defeated Union army retreated across the Rappahannock.

14. Union Army Observation Balloon Flown over Stafford Heights. An observer from the basket of the balloon could accurately direct Federal cannon fire into the defenders' lines at Fredericksburg. Several Confederate cannon shelled the balloon in an unsuccessful attempt to bring it down.

15. The Ruins of Fredericksburg after the Union Bombardment. The town suffered extensively from the Federal artillery bombardment. After the battle the soldiers of Lee's army donated money to assist the suffering population, many of whom were without housing or provisions.

16. The Union Army Retreats from Fredericksburg, December 13, 1862. The Federal army of forty thousand lost twelve thousand six hundred men to the Confederate defenders of Fredericksburg. When the Army of the Potomac retreated, Lee's army, which had lost over five thousand men, did not follow.

17. Nurses and Officers of the U.S. Sanitary Commission at Fredericksburg, Virginia. Most Civil War nurses were men, often convalescent soldiers, but some women served in military hospitals. The U.S. Sanitary Commission was a philanthropic organization that gave valuable assistance to the overworked army medical officers, who were especially taxed at Fredericksburg.

18. The Mud March, January 21, 1863. A month after the defeat at Fredericksburg, General Burnside sent the Army of the Potomac marching up the Rappahannock in an attempt to outflank the defenders of Richmond. The mud and flooding caused by heavy winter rains brought the army to a floundering halt, with cannon and wagons hopelessly stalled. General Burnside had failed again.

19. Ladies Visit the Camp of the Army of the Potomac, Winter 1863. With the army in winter quarters some of the more well-to-do officers had their wives and relatives visit them in camp. Sometimes a full-dress ball was given in honor of the ladies.

20. Confederate Camp, 1863. Southern soldiers enjoyed well-equipped camps like this only in the early years of the war. As equipment and supplies grew ever more scarce, the Confederates often had to make do without the luxury of tents and adequate food supplies.

21. Fugitive Slaves Entering the Union Lines, 1863. Runaway slaves of all ages flocked into the lines of the Union army whenever the Federals appeared in the neighborhood. They came carrying infants and their few possessions, in search of freedom. Many of the men were put to work by the U.S. government as laborers and teamsters, and many were recruited as soldiers.

22. The Union Army on the March to Chancellorsville, Virginia, April 1863.
General Joseph Hooker replaced Burnside as commander of the Army of the
Potomac in early 1863. With an army of one hundred thirty-four thousand men,
Hooker advanced through the Virginia Wilderness toward Chancellorsville.

23. General Joseph Hooker, U.S.A., 1863. Nicknamed "Fighting Joe," Hooker had been a fine division and corps commander, and looked every inch a soldier, but he was a heavy drinker and, though a good administrator, he was vain and arrogant. His Southern adversary, General Lee, did not think much of him as an army commander.

24. Union Artillery at Chancellorsville. After advancing boldly to outflank the Army of Northern Virginia at Chancellorsville, Hooker suddenly delayed attacking and then, to the surprise of his officers, ordered his army to retreat to a defensive position. Union artillery at Chancellorsville could not operate effectively, since the terrain before them was marked by ravines and covered with dense thickets.

25. Jackson's Troops Attack Hooker's Flank at Chancellorsville. Lee ordered Stonewall Jackson's corps of twenty-eight thousand men to march around the right flank of the Federal army and launch a surprise attack. Jackson's men attacked Northern soldiers who were preparing dinner with their arms stacked, and drove them back in confusion.

26. Rescuing the Wounded from the Burning Woods at Chancellorsville. In the furious fighting that followed the attack upon the Union right, patches of woods around Chancellorsville caught fire and some of the wounded on both sides burned to death, despite efforts to rescue them.

27. Wounding of Stonewall Jackson, May 2, 1863. On the evening of this day of battle, Stonewall Jackson, accompanied by some couriers and guides, galloped eastward to inspect the terrain where the next day's fighting would occur. In the darkness, Confederate troops, believing Jackson's party to be Union cavalrymen, loosed a volley of rifle fire which wounded Jackson and killed several of his companions.

28. The House Where Stonewall Jackson Died, May 10, 1863.
Chancellorsville was Lee's greatest victory, ending in another
humiliating retreat for the Federal army, but the death of Stonewall
Jackson, from wounds received on the night of May 2, was the worst
disaster that had yet struck the Army of Northern Virginia. Jackson
died peacefully in this plantation house at Guinea Station, Virginia.

29. Punishment in the Federal Camp: Riding the Wooden Horse. The almost continuous series of defeats suffered by the Army of the Potomac had caused a general lowering of morale among the Northern troops. Regimental commanders resorted to disciplinary measures like the one shown for such minor offenses as drunkenness and insubordination.

30. Confederate Cavalry Charge Union Guns at Brandy Station. To screen his second invasion of the North from the Federals, Lee ordered his cavalry commander, Jeb Stuart, to establish a temporary headquarters at Brandy Station, Virginia, in order to block Union attempts at reconnaissance. On June 9, a Federal cavalry force almost captured Stuart's headquarters on Fleetwood Hill, but were driven back, in the biggest cavalry battle of the war.

31. General J. E. B. Stuart, Commander of Cavalry, Army of Northern Virginia. Jeb Stuart was called "the eyes of the army" because of his skill at gathering information for General Lee. Stuart briefly succeeded Stonewall Jackson as commander of the Second Army Corps after Jackson's death. The most famed of Confederate cavalry commanders, Stuart died in battle in 1864.

32. General Robert E. Lee, Army of Northern Virginia. Lee was now at the height of his success. After defeating the first Union attempt to capture Richmond in the Seven Days Battles on the Peninsula, earlier in 1862, Lee had now fought a drawn battle at Antietam in Maryland, and gained two brilliant successes at Fredericksburg and Chancellorsville. One more such victory might bring the recognition and assistance of Great Britain and other European powers to the hard-pressed Southern cause. Lee resolved to seek that victory in Pennsylvania.

33. Lee's Army Moves into Pennsylvania, June 1863. When the Army of Northern Virginia reached Pennsylvania the various infantry corps spread out across the country, from Chambersburg to York, and north to Carlisle, searching for food and supplies. On June 28, Lee learned that the Union army was approaching his positions and he began concentrating his army around Gettysburg.

34. Reveille in Union Camp. The Union army had not opposed Lee's northern advance through Maryland. General Hooker, in a dispute with Washington, requested to be relieved of his command, and was replaced by General George G. Meade, while the Federal army slowly followed Lee into Pennsylvania. In this scene, two drummer boys and a bugler rouse the sleeping men of the Army of the Potomac at dawn.

35. Death of General John F. Reynolds at Gettysburg, July 1, 1863. Near Cashtown, Pennsylvania, the advance units of a Union cavalry division happened, by accident, upon the Southern army. Though outnumbered, the Northern cavalrymen dismounted and fought a delaying action. Union corps commander General John F. Reynolds rushed reinforcements to the hard-pressed Federal cavalrymen and was shot down by Confederate riflemen as he advanced.

36. First Day's Fighting around Gettysburg, July 1, 1863, near the McPherson Barn. General Meade sent his First and Eleventh Corps into the battle, but Lee's Second Corps came down upon them and drove the Federals back through Gettysburg. Union casualties were heavy in the desperate, hand-to-hand fighting. The Twenty-fourth Michigan regiment lost 399 of its 496 men on this day.

37. Fighting at Devil's Den, July 2, 1863. The retreating Federals formed into a very strong line, holding the key positions of Culp's Hill, Cemetery Hill, Cemetery Ridge and Little Round Top. Some of the most severe fighting of the second day's battle was at Devil's Den, where the Texans of Hood's Confederate brigade fought all day over the boulder-strewn, desolate ground. At day's end the Union army held all of its positions and Lee's veterans had taken heavy casualties.

38. General John B. Hood, Army of Northern Virginia. A West Pointer and former U.S. Army officer, Hood commanded the Texas Brigade in Lee's army and rose to the rank of major general before being sent, after Gettysburg, to the West, where he lost a leg in the battle of Chickamauga.

39. Confederate Artillery at Gettysburg, July 3, 1863. After having tried to break the Union right and left without success, Lee tried to force the center of the Union line on the afternoon of July 3. His attack was preceded by a Confederate artillery bombardment which was meant to silence the cannons of the Federal army, but the Southerners simply did not have enough guns or shells.

40. Pickett Attacks the Union Center on Cemetery Ridge, July 3, 1863.
Confederate General George E. Pickett led a frontal assault on the center
of the Union line along a mile of the front. The Southerners advanced
through shellfire from massed Union cannon, and though decimated,
some of the attackers actually broke through a portion of the Union line
on Cemetery Ridge, but could not hold the positions they had won.

41. General George E. Pickett, Army of Northern Virginia. Another West Pointer and former U.S. Army officer who joined the Confederacy, Pickett is best remembered for the disastrous charge he led at Gettysburg. Nearly six thousand of the Virginians and North Carolinians he led up Cemetery Ridge remained casualties on the field.

42. Lee Meets the Survivors of Pickett's Charge, July 3, 1863. As the survivors of the failed attack made their way wearily back over the ground littered with the bodies of their dead and wounded, they saw General Lee riding out to them. "It was all my fault," Lee told them. "We must all stand together now, to save the rest."

43. Confederate Prisoners Taken at Gettysburg. On July 4 the Confederate army began its last retreat back into Virginia. Never again would Lee have the strength or opportunity to mount another such offensive. Behind them the Southerners left almost four thousand men dead and over five thousand prisoners or missing.

44. General George G. Meade, U.S.A. The victor of Gettysburg, Meade was a professional soldier and an expert tactician. He was criticized by many for not pursuing the defeated Army of Northern Virginia after the battle and attacking Lee before he could take up defensive positions on his home ground.

45. Cavalry Battle at Boonsboro, Maryland, during the Confederate Retreat from Gettysburg. As Lee retreated, Jeb Stuart, with four brigades of cavalry, struck the right and rear of the Union line. General George A. Custer met him in a swirling cavalry battle which ended in a draw. The Gettysburg campaign had ended in defeat for the Confederates.

DOVER COLORING BOOKS

FAVORITE ROSES COLORING BOOK, Ilil Arbel. (25845-9) $2.95

FUN WITH SEARCH-A-WORD COLORING BOOK, Nina Barbaresi. (26327-4) $2.50

FUN WITH SPELLING COLORING BOOK, Nina Barbaresi. (25999-4) $2.50

JEWISH HOLIDAYS AND TRADITIONS COLORING BOOK, Chaya Burstein. (26322-3) $2.95

INDIAN TRIBES OF NORTH AMERICA COLORING BOOK, Peter F. Copeland. (26303-7) $2.95

BIRDS OF PREY COLORING BOOK, John Green. (25989-7) $2.95

LIFE IN ANCIENT EGYPT COLORING BOOK, John Green and Stanley Appelbaum. (26130-1) $2.95

WHALES AND DOLPHINS COLORING BOOK, John Green. (26306-1) $2.95

DINOSAUR ABC COLORING BOOK, Llyn Hunter. (25786-X) $2.50

SHARKS OF THE WORLD COLORING BOOK, Llyn Hunter. (26137-9) $2.95

HISTORY OF SPACE EXPLORATION COLORING BOOK, Bruce LaFontaine. (26152-2) $2.95

HOLIDAYS STAINED GLASS COLORING BOOK, Ted Menten. (26062-3) $3.95

FUN WITH OPPOSITES COLORING BOOK, Anna Pomaska and Suzanne Ross. (25983-8) $2.50

DINOSAUR LIFE ACTIVITY BOOK, Donald Silver and Patricia Wynne. (25809-2) $2.50

HISTORY OF THE AMERICAN AUTOMOBILE COLORING BOOK, A. G. Smith and Randy Mason. (26315-0) $2.95

THE VELVETEEN RABBIT COLORING BOOK, Margery Williams and Thea Kliros. (25924-2) $2.95

HEBREW ALPHABET COLORING BOOK, Chaya Burstein. (25089-X) $2.95

COLUMBUS DISCOVERS AMERICA COLORING BOOK, Peter F. Copeland. (25542-5) $2.75

STORY OF THE AMERICAN REVOLUTION COLORING BOOK, Peter Copeland. (25648-0) $2.95

FAVORITE POEMS FOR CHILDREN COLORING BOOK, illustrated by Susan Gaber. (23923-3) $2.95

HORSES OF THE WORLD COLORING BOOK, John Green. (24985-9) $2.95

WILD ANIMALS COLORING BOOK, John Green. (25476-3) $2.95

THE DAYS OF THE DINOSAUR COLORING BOOK, MATTHEW KALMENOFF. (25359-7) $2.95

SMALL ANIMALS OF NORTH AMERICA COLORING BOOK, Elizabeth A. McClelland. (24217-X) $2.95

Paperbound unless otherwise indicated. Prices subject to change without notice. Available at your book dealer or write for free catalogues to Dept. 23, Dover Publications, Inc., 31 East 2nd Street, Mineola, N.Y. 11501. Please indicate field of interest. Each year Dover publishes over 200 books on fine art, music, crafts and needlework, antiques, languages, literature, children's books, chess, cookery, nature, anthropology, science, mathematics, and other areas.

Manufactured in the U.S.A.